How a tadpole grows into a frog

Written by
David Stewart

Illustrated by
Carolyn Franklin

croak

croak!

Hold the page
up to the light
and see if you
can see the
frog's skeleton.

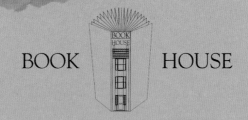
BOOK HOUSE

Published in Great Britain in 2007 by
Book House, an imprint of
The Salariya Book Company Ltd
25 Marlborough Place, Brighton BN1 1UB

SALARIYA

HB ISBN 978-1-905087-21-1
PB ISBN 978-1-905087-22-8

Visit our website at **www.book-house.co.uk**
for free electronic versions of:
You Wouldn't Want to be an Egyptian Mummy!
You Wouldn't Want to be a Roman Gladiator!
Avoid Joining Shackleton's Polar Expedition!
Avoid Sailing on a 19th-Century Whaling Ship!

Author: David Stewart has written many non-fiction
books for children on historical topics, including *You Wouldn't
Want to be an Egyptian Mummy!* and *Avoid Sailing on the
Titanic!* He lives in Brighton, England, with his wife and son.

Artist: Carolyn Franklin is a graduate of Brighton
College of Art, England, specialising in design and illustration.
She has worked in animation, advertising and children's fiction
and non-fiction. She has a particular interest in natural history
and has written many books on the subject, including *Life in
the Wetlands* in the WHAT ON EARTH? series and *Egg to Owl*
in the CYCLES OF LIFE series.

Consultant: Monica Hughes is an experienced
Educational Advisor and author of more than one hundred
books for young children. She has been Headteacher of a First
School, Primary Advisory Teacher and Senior Lecturer in Early
Childhood Education.

A catalogue record for this book is available from
the British Library.

Printed and bound in China.

Contents

What *is* a frog?

A frog begins life as an egg. A **tadpole** hatches from the egg. The tadpole slowly grows into a small frog called a **froglet**, and then it becomes an **adult** frog.

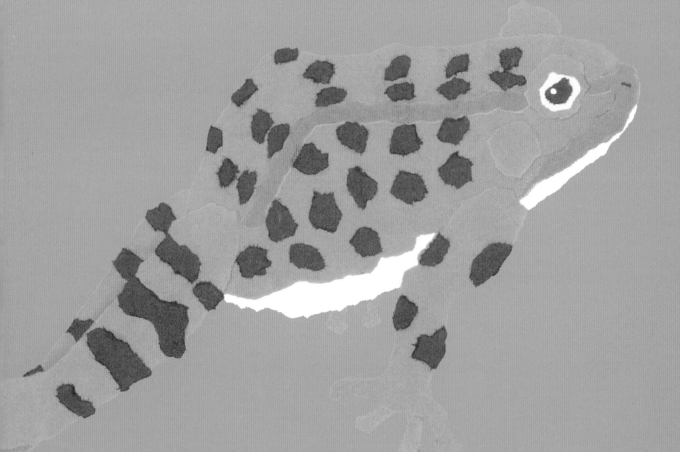

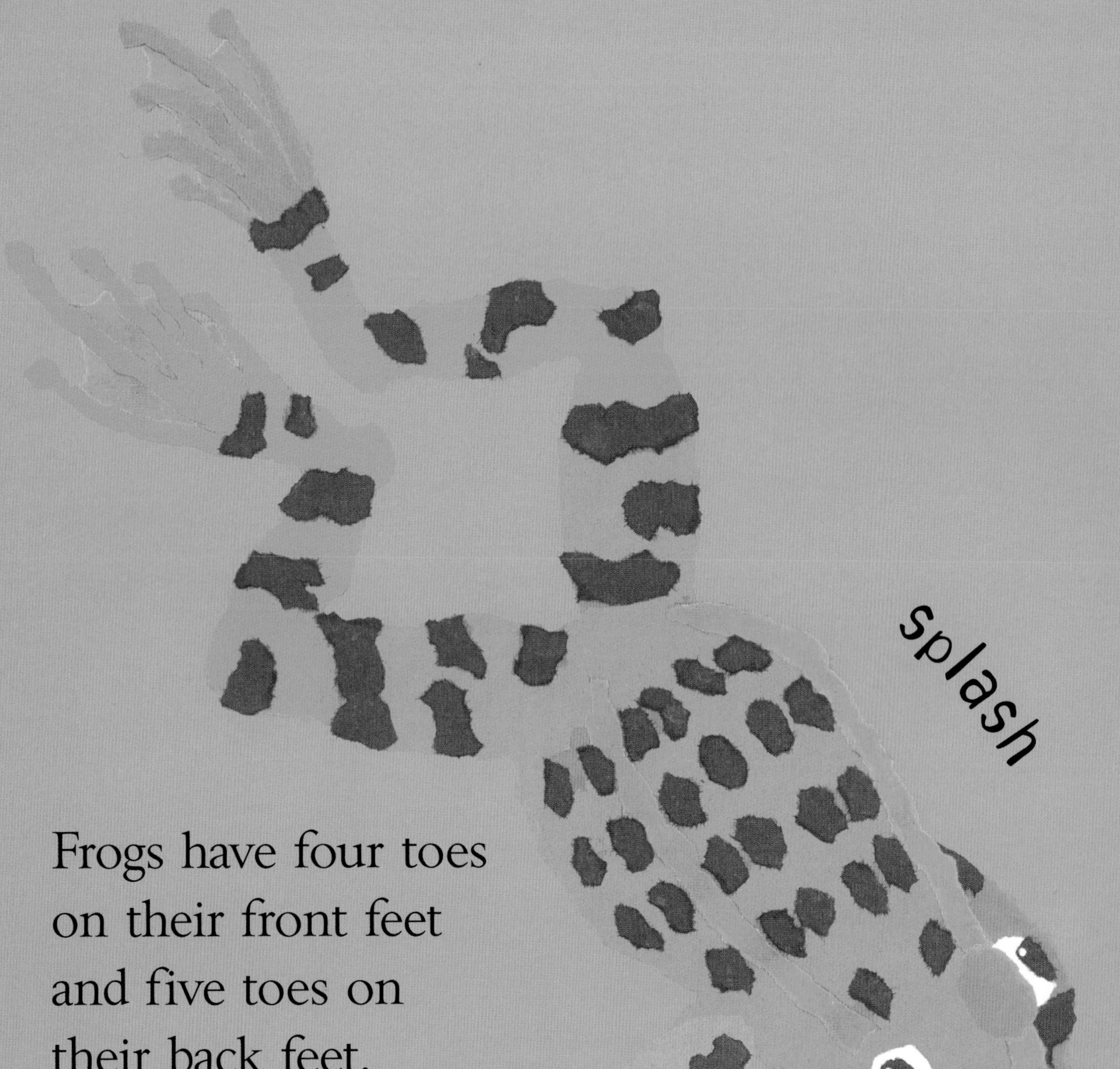

five toes

splash

Frogs have four toes
on their front feet
and five toes on
their back feet.

splash

splash

four toes

5

Where do frogs live?

Frogs live some of the time in ponds and streams. They also live on land, in the grassy damp areas near to water. Creatures that live both in water and also on land are called **amphibians**.

dragonfly

water lily

bulrushes

There are a lot of frogs in this pond. One frog is sitting on a lily pad and another frog is jumping.

croak
croak

lily pad

7

What sounds do frogs make?

In the spring, frogs look for a partner. The male frog calls to a female frog. He makes the sides of his throat swell up and croaks very loudly so that she will notice him.

croak
croak
croak

grunt

chirp
chirp
chirp

The female frog then
answers him in grunts
and chirps.

9

Do frogs lay eggs?

When the male has found a female, the two frogs mate. The female frog lays about three thousand eggs. Then the male frog covers the eggs with **sperm**. This **fertilises** the eggs and they begin to grow.

splash Splash
splash

splash

splash

As the eggs start to grow, they
stick together. The eggs are now
called **frogspawn**.

frogspawn

11

What are tadpoles?

Each egg grows inside a tiny ball of jelly. See how the eggs start to change shape. As they grow larger, they grow a head and a tail.

egg

head

tail

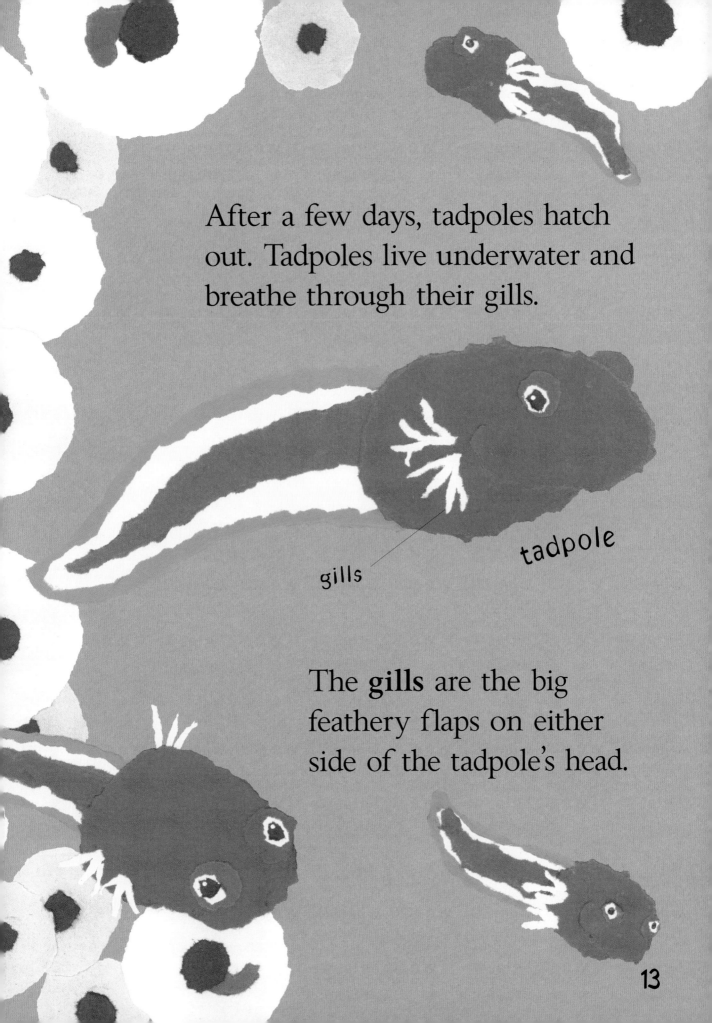

After a few days, tadpoles hatch out. Tadpoles live underwater and breathe through their gills.

gills

tadpole

The **gills** are the big feathery flaps on either side of the tadpole's head.

What do tadpoles eat?

At first tadpoles eat only tiny water plants. As they get bigger they start to eat small creatures such as water fleas and pond worms.

munch munch

small back legs

As it grows bigger
and bigger, the
tadpole starts to grow
back legs.

What happens to the tadpole's tail?

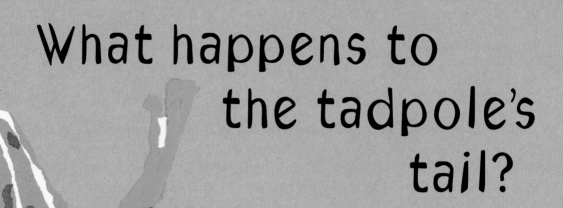

front
legs

The tadpole's tail gets smaller and smaller. Soon it starts to grow two front legs. It is now starting to look like a frog.

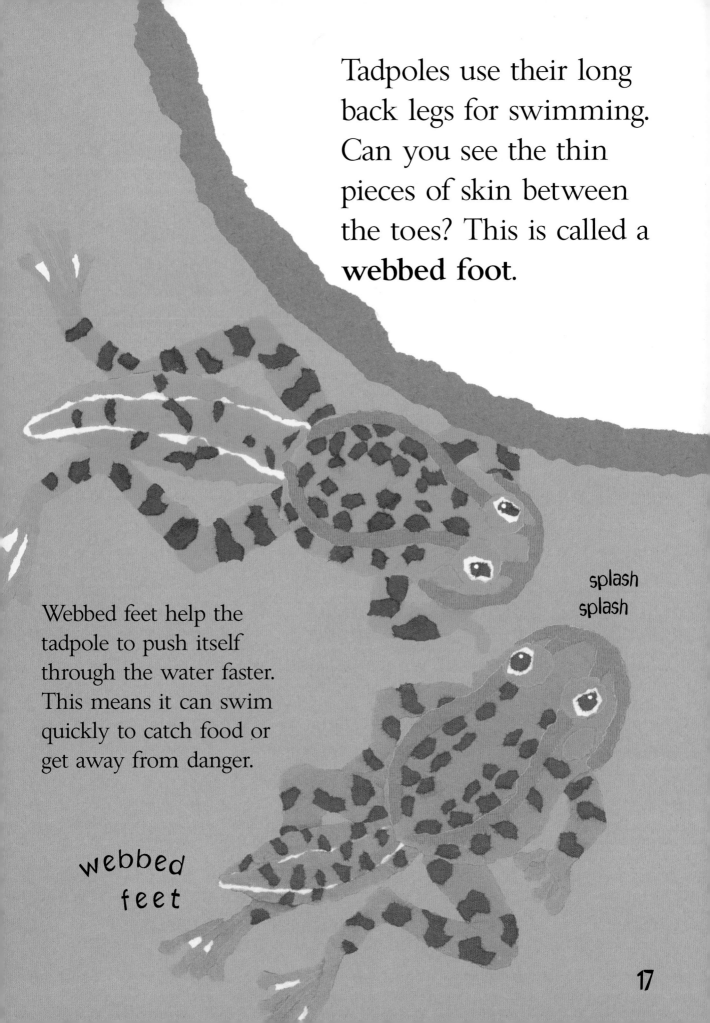

Tadpoles use their long back legs for swimming. Can you see the thin pieces of skin between the toes? This is called a **webbed foot**.

Webbed feet help the tadpole to push itself through the water faster. This means it can swim quickly to catch food or get away from danger.

splash
splash

webbed feet

Can the froglets breathe air?

The tadpoles have now grown into young frogs which are called **froglets**. The froglets can put their heads out of the water and breathe air.

croak
croak

See how small the tail is now!

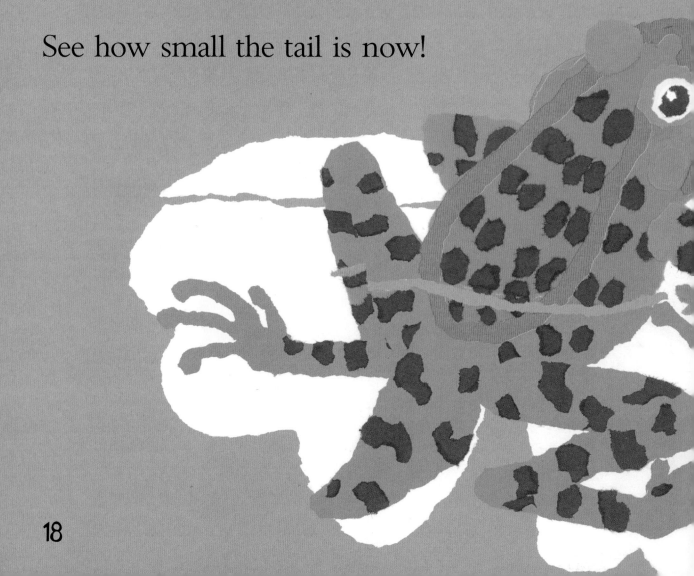

damselfly

These froglets will soon leave the water and live on land. They have stopped using their gills and started to use their **lungs** to breathe.

splash

splash

What do froglets eat?

The froglets climb out of the water to look for food. They like to eat slugs and snails.

snail

insect

gulp

gulp

Frogs and froglets have long,
sticky tongues that are good
for catching insects.

slug

What dangers do froglets face?

Cats like to chase froglets. Many other creatures like to eat them. The froglets must quickly jump away and try to hide from danger.

croak
croak

croak
croak

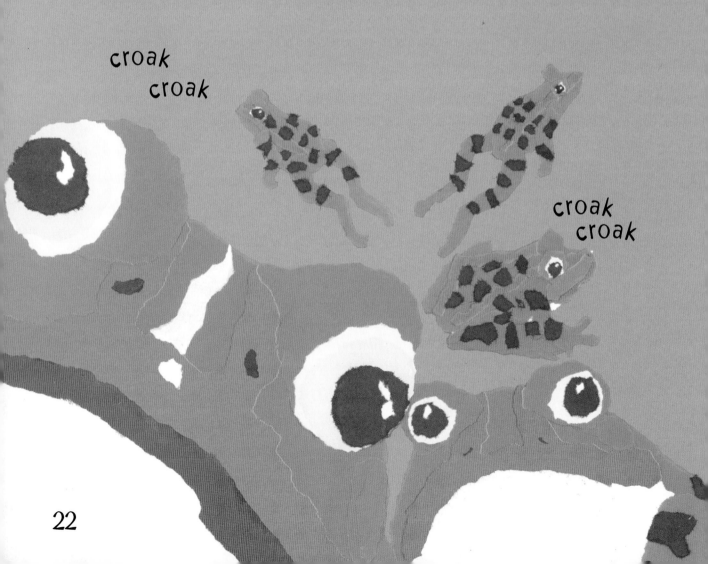

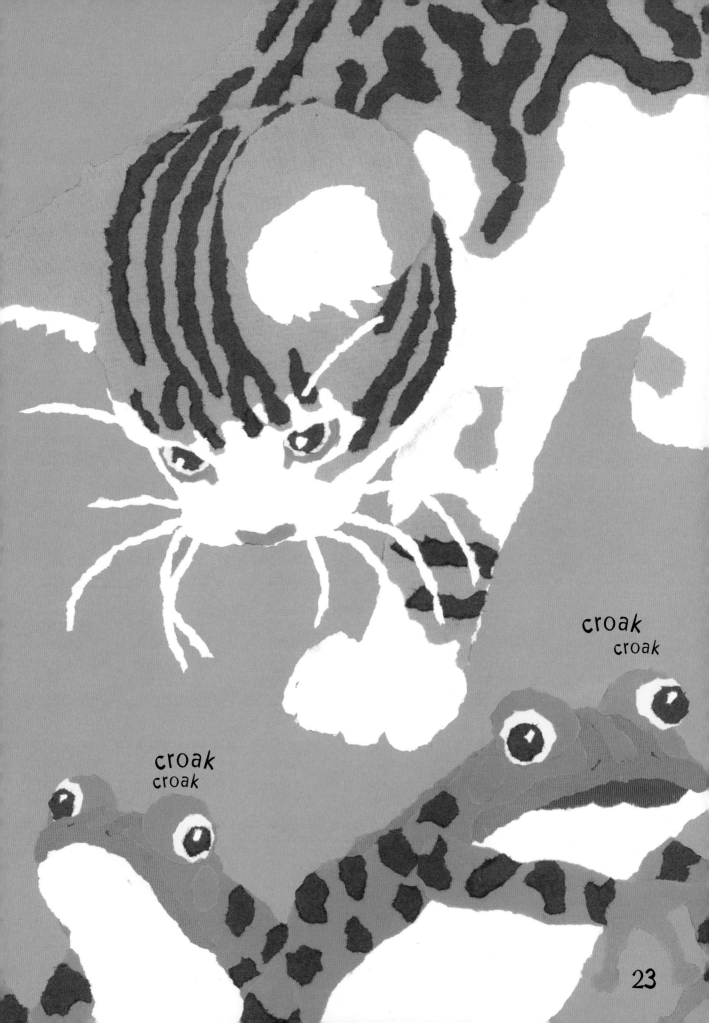

croak
croak

croak
croak

How long does it take for a froglet to grow into a frog?

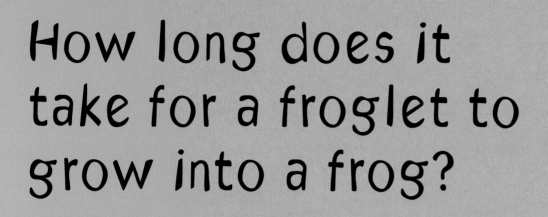

Slowly the froglets grow into **adult** frogs. After three years the adult male frog will look for a mate. Then the female frog will lay eggs and the cycle of life will begin again.

croak
croak

Things to do

How to look inside a pond

You will need:

One large clear plastic bottle

Scissors

Sticky tape

Transparent kitchen film

1 Ask an adult to cut off the top and bottom of the bottle.

2 Carefully tape a piece of transparent kitchen film to the base of the bottle.

3 Put the covered end of the bottle just below the surface of the pond. Look down into the other end.

26

How does it work?

It is usually very difficult to see into a pond because the top of the water is very shiny and reflects light. By using this tube to look through the water, you can look straight down and see what is underneath the surface.

What can you see under the water?

Where do frogs go in the winter?

When it starts to get cold, adult frogs **hibernate**. They hide under a pile of mud and leaves at the bottom of the pond and go to sleep.

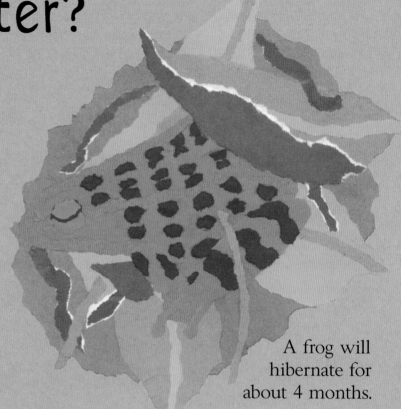

A frog will hibernate for about 4 months.

Keep a frog diary

My Frog Diary

Date: 6th March

I saw lots of frogspawn.

Date: 13th March

In early spring, visit your local pond every few days to look out for frogspawn. A week later, look for tadpoles. Each time you visit the pond, write down the date and what you have seen.

A frog's year

Winter

The frog hibernates. It will wake up for a short while, then go back to sleep.

Winter/Spring

The frog has woken up. It goes to find a mate.

Spring

The female frog lays her eggs. Tadpoles start to hatch out.

Spring

More and more tadpoles hatch out. The tadpoles feed and grow bigger.

Spring

Tadpoles grow back legs. Their tails get smaller. Then they grow front legs.

Summer

Some of the tiny froglets leave the pond.

Summer

The other froglets leave the pond.

Summer

The adult frog lives in long grass.

Autumn

Froglets eat lots of food. Their body stores the food and they grow fat.

Autumn

As it gets colder, the frog finds a place to hibernate.

Autumn

Some of the young frogs are still looking for food.

Winter

Most of the frogs are hibernating. Frogs often wake up for a short time to feed.

29

* These are approximate times. Each frog lives in a different habitat and has its own timescale.

How a frog grows

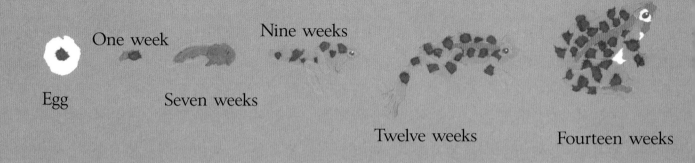

One week

Nine weeks

Egg

Seven weeks

Twelve weeks

Fourteen weeks

Words to remember

Adult Grown-up

Amphibians Creatures able to live in water or on land. They begin their lives in water.

Froglet A young frog.

Fertilisation When an egg and a sperm join together.

Frogspawn The sticky mass of eggs that floats on the surface of the water. Tadpoles hatch from frogspawn.

Gills These are needed by creatures to breathe underwater. They are on the outside of the body.

Twenty weeks

Fully grown

Hibernate To go to sleep during the winter.

Lungs These are needed by creatures to breathe air. They are inside the body.

Sperm The liquid from the male that joins the egg from the female to produce a baby.

Tadpole The small creature that hatches from a frog's egg.

Webbed feet Feet with stretched skin between the toes. Webbed feet help frogs to swim.

Index